Federal Register

Vol. 75, No. 2

Tuesday, January 5, 2010

Presidential Documents

Title 3—

The President

Executive Order 13526: **Classified National**

Security Information

This order prescribes a uniform system for classifying, safeguarding, and declassifying national security information, including information relating to defense against transnational terrorism. Our democratic principles require that the American people be informed of the activities of their Government. Also, our Nation's progress depends on the free flow of information both within the Government and to the American people. Nevertheless, throughout our history, the national defense has required that certain information be maintained in confidence in order to protect our citizens, our democratic institutions, our homeland security, and our interactions with foreign nations. Protecting information critical to our Nation's security and demonstrating our commitment to open Government through accurate and accountable application of classification standards and routine, secure, and effective declassification are equally important priorities.

NOW, THEREFORE, I, BARACK OBAMA, by the authority vested in me as President by the Constitution and the laws of the United States of America, it is hereby ordered as follows:

PART 1—ORIGINAL CLASSIFICATION

Section 1.1. *Classification Standards.* (a) Information may be originally classified under the terms of this order only if all of the following conditions are met:

(1) an original classification authority is classifying the information;

(2) the information is owned by, produced by or for, or is under the control of the United States Government;

(3) the information falls within one or more of the categories of information listed in section 1.4 of this order; and

(4) the original classification authority determines that the unauthorized disclosure of the information reasonably could be expected to result in damage to the national security, which includes defense against transnational terrorism, and the original classification authority is able to identify or describe the damage.

(b) If there is significant doubt about the need to classify information, it shall not be classified. This provision does not:

(1) amplify or modify the substantive criteria or procedures for classification; or

(2) create any substantive or procedural rights subject to judicial review.

(c) Classified information shall not be declassified automatically as a result of any unauthorized disclosure of identical or similar information.

(d) The unauthorized disclosure of foreign government information is presumed to cause damage to the national security.

Sec. 1.2. *Classification Levels.* (a) Information may be classified at one of the following three levels:

(1) "Top Secret" shall be applied to information, the unauthorized disclosure of which reasonably could be expected to cause exceptionally grave damage to the national security that the original classification authority is able to identify or describe.

(2) "Secret" shall be applied to information, the unauthorized disclosure of which reasonably could be expected to cause serious damage to the

national security that the original classification authority is able to identify or describe.

(3) "Confidential" shall be applied to information, the unauthorized disclosure of which reasonably could be expected to cause damage to the national security that the original classification authority is able to identify or describe.

(b) Except as otherwise provided by statute, no other terms shall be used to identify United States classified information.

(c) If there is significant doubt about the appropriate level of classification, it shall be classified at the lower level.

Sec. 1.3. *Classification Authority.* (a) The authority to classify information originally may be exercised only by:

(1) the President and the Vice President;

(2) agency heads and officials designated by the President; and

(3) United States Government officials delegated this authority pursuant to paragraph (c) of this section.

(b) Officials authorized to classify information at a specified level are also authorized to classify information at a lower level.

(c) Delegation of original classification authority.

(1) Delegations of original classification authority shall be limited to the minimum required to administer this order. Agency heads are responsible for ensuring that designated subordinate officials have a demonstrable and continuing need to exercise this authority.

(2) "Top Secret" original classification authority may be delegated only by the President, the Vice President, or an agency head or official designated pursuant to paragraph (a)(2) of this section.

(3) "Secret" or "Confidential" original classification authority may be delegated only by the President, the Vice President, an agency head or official designated pursuant to paragraph (a)(2) of this section, or the senior agency official designated under section 5.4(d) of this order, provided that official has been delegated "Top Secret" original classification authority by the agency head.

(4) Each delegation of original classification authority shall be in writing and the authority shall not be redelegated except as provided in this order. Each delegation shall identify the official by name or position.

(5) Delegations of original classification authority shall be reported or made available by name or position to the Director of the Information Security Oversight Office.

(d) All original classification authorities must receive training in proper classification (including the avoidance of over-classification) and declassification as provided in this order and its implementing directives at least once a calendar year. Such training must include instruction on the proper safeguarding of classified information and on the sanctions in section 5.5 of this order that may be brought against an individual who fails to classify information properly or protect classified information from unauthorized disclosure. Original classification authorities who do not receive such mandatory training at least once within a calendar year shall have their classification authority suspended by the agency head or the senior agency official designated under section 5.4(d) of this order until such training has taken place. A waiver may be granted by the agency head, the deputy agency head, or the senior agency official if an individual is unable to receive such training due to unavoidable circumstances. Whenever a waiver is granted, the individual shall receive such training as soon as practicable.

(e) Exceptional cases. When an employee, government contractor, licensee, certificate holder, or grantee of an agency who does not have original classification authority originates information believed by that person to require classification, the information shall be protected in a manner consistent with this order and its implementing directives. The information shall be transmitted promptly as provided under this order or its implementing directives to the agency that has appropriate subject matter interest and classification authority with respect to this information. That agency shall decide within 30 days whether to classify this information.

Sec. 1.4. *Classification Categories.* Information shall not be considered for classification unless its unauthorized disclosure could reasonably be expected to cause identifiable or describable damage to the national security in accordance with section 1.2 of this order, and it pertains to one or more of the following:

(a) military plans, weapons systems, or operations;

(b) foreign government information;

(c) intelligence activities (including covert action), intelligence sources or methods, or cryptology;

(d) foreign relations or foreign activities of the United States, including confidential sources;

(e) scientific, technological, or economic matters relating to the national security;

(f) United States Government programs for safeguarding nuclear materials or facilities;

(g) vulnerabilities or capabilities of systems, installations, infrastructures, projects, plans, or protection services relating to the national security; or

(h) the development, production, or use of weapons of mass destruction.

Sec. 1.5. *Duration of Classification.* (a) At the time of original classification, the original classification authority shall establish a specific date or event for declassification based on the duration of the national security sensitivity of the information. Upon reaching the date or event, the information shall be automatically declassified. Except for information that should clearly and demonstrably be expected to reveal the identity of a confidential human source or a human intelligence source or key design concepts of weapons of mass destruction, the date or event shall not exceed the time frame established in paragraph (b) of this section.

(b) If the original classification authority cannot determine an earlier specific date or event for declassification, information shall be marked for declassification 10 years from the date of the original decision, unless the original classification authority otherwise determines that the sensitivity of the information requires that it be marked for declassification for up to 25 years from the date of the original decision.

(c) An original classification authority may extend the duration of classification up to 25 years from the date of origin of the document, change the level of classification, or reclassify specific information only when the standards and procedures for classifying information under this order are followed.

(d) No information may remain classified indefinitely. Information marked for an indefinite duration of classification under predecessor orders, for example, marked as "Originating Agency's Determination Required," or classified information that contains incomplete declassification instructions or lacks declassification instructions shall be declassified in accordance with part 3 of this order.

Sec. 1.6. *Identification and Markings.* (a) At the time of original classification, the following shall be indicated in a manner that is immediately apparent:

(1) one of the three classification levels defined in section 1.2 of this order;

(2) the identity, by name and position, or by personal identifier, of the original classification authority;

(3) the agency and office of origin, if not otherwise evident;

(4) declassification instructions, which shall indicate one of the following:

(A) the date or event for declassification, as prescribed in section 1.5(a);

(B) the date that is 10 years from the date of original classification, as prescribed in section 1.5(b);

(C) the date that is up to 25 years from the date of original classification, as prescribed in section 1.5(b); or

(D) in the case of information that should clearly and demonstrably be expected to reveal the identity of a confidential human source or a human intelligence source or key design concepts of weapons of mass destruction, the marking prescribed in implementing directives issued pursuant to this order; and

(5) a concise reason for classification that, at a minimum, cites the applicable classification categories in section 1.4 of this order.

(b) Specific information required in paragraph (a) of this section may be excluded if it would reveal additional classified information.

(c) With respect to each classified document, the agency originating the document shall, by marking or other means, indicate which portions are classified, with the applicable classification level, and which portions are unclassified. In accordance with standards prescribed in directives issued under this order, the Director of the Information Security Oversight Office may grant and revoke temporary waivers of this requirement. The Director shall revoke any waiver upon a finding of abuse.

(d) Markings or other indicia implementing the provisions of this order, including abbreviations and requirements to safeguard classified working papers, shall conform to the standards prescribed in implementing directives issued pursuant to this order.

(e) Foreign government information shall retain its original classification markings or shall be assigned a U.S. classification that provides a degree of protection at least equivalent to that required by the entity that furnished the information. Foreign government information retaining its original classification markings need not be assigned a U.S. classification marking provided that the responsible agency determines that the foreign government markings are adequate to meet the purposes served by U.S. classification markings.

(f) Information assigned a level of classification under this or predecessor orders shall be considered as classified at that level of classification despite the omission of other required markings. Whenever such information is used in the derivative classification process or is reviewed for possible declassification, holders of such information shall coordinate with an appropriate classification authority for the application of omitted markings.

(g) The classification authority shall, whenever practicable, use a classified addendum whenever classified information constitutes a small portion of an otherwise unclassified document or prepare a product to allow for dissemination at the lowest level of classification possible or in unclassified form.

(h) Prior to public release, all declassified records shall be appropriately marked to reflect their declassification.

Sec. 1.7. *Classification Prohibitions and Limitations.* (a) In no case shall information be classified, continue to be maintained as classified, or fail to be declassified in order to:

(1) conceal violations of law, inefficiency, or administrative error;

(2) prevent embarrassment to a person, organization, or agency;

(3) restrain competition; or

(4) prevent or delay the release of information that does not require protection in the interest of the national security.

(b) Basic scientific research information not clearly related to the national security shall not be classified.

(c) Information may not be reclassified after declassification and release to the public under proper authority unless:

(1) the reclassification is personally approved in writing by the agency head based on a document-by-document determination by the agency that reclassification is required to prevent significant and demonstrable damage to the national security;

(2) the information may be reasonably recovered without bringing undue attention to the information;

(3) the reclassification action is reported promptly to the Assistant to the President for National Security Affairs (National Security Advisor) and the Director of the Information Security Oversight Office; and

(4) for documents in the physical and legal custody of the National Archives and Records Administration (National Archives) that have been available for public use, the agency head has, after making the determinations required by this paragraph, notified the Archivist of the United States (Archivist), who shall suspend public access pending approval of the reclassification action by the Director of the Information Security Oversight Office. Any such decision by the Director may be appealed by the agency head to the President through the National Security Advisor. Public access shall remain suspended pending a prompt decision on the appeal.

(d) Information that has not previously been disclosed to the public under proper authority may be classified or reclassified after an agency has received a request for it under the Freedom of Information Act (5 U.S.C. 552), the Presidential Records Act, 44 U.S.C. 2204(c)(1), the Privacy Act of 1974 (5 U.S.C. 552a), or the mandatory review provisions of section 3.5 of this order only if such classification meets the requirements of this order and is accomplished on a document-by-document basis with the personal participation or under the direction of the agency head, the deputy agency head, or the senior agency official designated under section 5.4 of this order. The requirements in this paragraph also apply to those situations in which information has been declassified in accordance with a specific date or event determined by an original classification authority in accordance with section 1.5 of this order.

(e) Compilations of items of information that are individually unclassified may be classified if the compiled information reveals an additional association or relationship that:

(1) meets the standards for classification under this order; and

(2) is not otherwise revealed in the individual items of information.

Sec. 1.8. *Classification Challenges.* (a) Authorized holders of information who, in good faith, believe that its classification status is improper are encouraged and expected to challenge the classification status of the information in accordance with agency procedures established under paragraph (b) of this section.

(b) In accordance with implementing directives issued pursuant to this order, an agency head or senior agency official shall establish procedures under which authorized holders of information, including authorized holders outside the classifying agency, are encouraged and expected to challenge the classification of information that they believe is improperly classified or unclassified. These procedures shall ensure that:

(1) individuals are not subject to retribution for bringing such actions;

(2) an opportunity is provided for review by an impartial official or panel; and

(3) individuals are advised of their right to appeal agency decisions to the Interagency Security Classification Appeals Panel (Panel) established by section 5.3 of this order.

(c) Documents required to be submitted for prepublication review or other administrative process pursuant to an approved nondisclosure agreement are not covered by this section.

Sec. 1.9. *Fundamental Classification Guidance Review.* (a) Agency heads shall complete on a periodic basis a comprehensive review of the agency's classification guidance, particularly classification guides, to ensure the guidance reflects current circumstances and to identify classified information that no longer requires protection and can be declassified. The initial fundamental classification guidance review shall be completed within 2 years of the effective date of this order.

(b) The classification guidance review shall include an evaluation of classified information to determine if it meets the standards for classification under section 1.4 of this order, taking into account an up-to-date assessment of likely damage as described under section 1.2 of this order.

(c) The classification guidance review shall include original classification authorities and agency subject matter experts to ensure a broad range of perspectives.

(d) Agency heads shall provide a report summarizing the results of the classification guidance review to the Director of the Information Security Oversight Office and shall release an unclassified version of this report to the public.

PART 2—DERIVATIVE CLASSIFICATION

Sec. 2.1. *Use of Derivative Classification.* (a) Persons who reproduce, extract, or summarize classified information, or who apply classification markings derived from source material or as directed by a classification guide, need not possess original classification authority.

(b) Persons who apply derivative classification markings shall:

(1) be identified by name and position, or by personal identifier, in a manner that is immediately apparent for each derivative classification action;

(2) observe and respect original classification decisions; and

(3) carry forward to any newly created documents the pertinent classification markings. For information derivatively classified based on multiple sources, the derivative classifier shall carry forward:

(A) the date or event for declassification that corresponds to the longest period of classification among the sources, or the marking established pursuant to section 1.6(a)(4)(D) of this order; and

(B) a listing of the source materials.

(c) Derivative classifiers shall, whenever practicable, use a classified addendum whenever classified information constitutes a small portion of an otherwise unclassified document or prepare a product to allow for dissemination at the lowest level of classification possible or in unclassified form.

(d) Persons who apply derivative classification markings shall receive training in the proper application of the derivative classification principles of the order, with an emphasis on avoiding over-classification, at least once every 2 years. Derivative classifiers who do not receive such training at least once every 2 years shall have their authority to apply derivative classification markings suspended until they have received such training. A waiver may be granted by the agency head, the deputy agency head, or the senior agency official if an individual is unable to receive such training due to unavoidable circumstances. Whenever a waiver is granted, the individual shall receive such training as soon as practicable.

Sec. 2.2. *Classification Guides.* (a) Agencies with original classification authority shall prepare classification guides to facilitate the proper and uniform derivative classification of information. These guides shall conform to standards contained in directives issued under this order.

(b) Each guide shall be approved personally and in writing by an official who:

(1) has program or supervisory responsibility over the information or is the senior agency official; and

(2) is authorized to classify information originally at the highest level of classification prescribed in the guide.

(c) Agencies shall establish procedures to ensure that classification guides are reviewed and updated as provided in directives issued under this order.

(d) Agencies shall incorporate original classification decisions into classification guides on a timely basis and in accordance with directives issued under this order.

(e) Agencies may incorporate exemptions from automatic declassification approved pursuant to section 3.3(j) of this order into classification guides, provided that the Panel is notified of the intent to take such action for specific information in advance of approval and the information remains in active use.

(f) The duration of classification of a document classified by a derivative classifier using a classification guide shall not exceed 25 years from the date of the origin of the document, except for:

(1) information that should clearly and demonstrably be expected to reveal the identity of a confidential human source or a human intelligence source or key design concepts of weapons of mass destruction; and

(2) specific information incorporated into classification guides in accordance with section 2.2(e) of this order.

PART 3—DECLASSIFICATION AND DOWNGRADING

Sec. 3.1. *Authority for Declassification.* (a) Information shall be declassified as soon as it no longer meets the standards for classification under this order.

(b) Information shall be declassified or downgraded by:

(1) the official who authorized the original classification, if that official is still serving in the same position and has original classification authority;

(2) the originator's current successor in function, if that individual has original classification authority;

(3) a supervisory official of either the originator or his or her successor in function, if the supervisory official has original classification authority; or (4) officials delegated declassification authority in writing by the agency head or the senior agency official of the originating agency.

(c) The Director of National Intelligence (or, if delegated by the Director of National Intelligence, the Principal Deputy Director of National Intelligence) may, with respect to the Intelligence Community, after consultation with the head of the originating Intelligence Community element or department, declassify, downgrade, or direct the declassification or downgrading of information or intelligence relating to intelligence sources, methods, or activities.

(d) It is presumed that information that continues to meet the classification requirements under this order requires continued protection. In some exceptional cases, however, the need to protect such information may be outweighed by the public interest in disclosure of the information, and in these cases the information should be declassified. When such questions arise, they shall be referred to the agency head or the senior agency official. That official will determine, as an exercise of discretion, whether the public interest in disclosure outweighs the damage to the national security that might reasonably be expected from disclosure. This provision does not:

(1) amplify or modify the substantive criteria or procedures for classification; or

(2) create any substantive or procedural rights subject to judicial review.

(e) If the Director of the Information Security Oversight Office determines that information is classified in violation of this order, the Director may require the information to be declassified by the agency that originated the classification. Any such decision by the Director may be appealed to the President through the National Security Advisor. The information shall remain classified pending a prompt decision on the appeal.

(f) The provisions of this section shall also apply to agencies that, under the terms of this order, do not have original classification authority, but had such authority under predecessor orders.

(g) No information may be excluded from declassification under section 3.3 of this order based solely on the type of document or record in which it is found. Rather, the classified information must be considered on the basis of its content.

(h) Classified nonrecord materials, including artifacts, shall be declassified as soon as they no longer meet the standards for classification under this order.

(i) When making decisions under sections 3.3, 3.4, and 3.5 of this order, agencies shall consider the final decisions of the Panel.

Sec. 3.2. *Transferred Records.*

(a) In the case of classified records transferred in conjunction with a transfer of functions, and not merely for storage purposes, the receiving agency shall be deemed to be the originating agency for purposes of this order.

(b) In the case of classified records that are not officially transferred as described in paragraph (a) of this section, but that originated in an agency that has ceased to exist and for which there is no successor agency, each agency in possession of such records shall be deemed to be the originating agency for purposes of this order. Such records may be declassified or downgraded by the agency in possession of the records after consultation with any other agency that has an interest in the subject matter of the records.

(c) Classified records accessioned into the National Archives shall be declassified or downgraded by the Archivist in accordance with this order, the directives issued pursuant to this order, agency declassification guides, and any existing procedural agreement between the Archivist and the relevant agency head.

(d) The originating agency shall take all reasonable steps to declassify classified information contained in records determined to have permanent historical value before they are accessioned into the National Archives. However, the Archivist may require that classified records be accessioned into the National Archives when necessary to comply with the provisions of the Federal Records Act. This provision does not apply to records transferred to the Archivist pursuant to section 2203 of title 44, United States Code, or records for which the National Archives serves as the custodian of the records of an agency or organization that has gone out of existence.

(e) To the extent practicable, agencies shall adopt a system of records management that will facilitate the public release of documents at the time such documents are declassified pursuant to the provisions for automatic declassification in section 3.3 of this order.

Sec. 3.3 *Automatic Declassification.*

(a) Subject to paragraphs (b)–(d) and (g)–(j) of this section, all classified records that (1) are more than 25 years old and (2) have been determined to have permanent historical value under title 44, United States Code, shall be automatically declassified whether or not the records have been reviewed. All classified records shall be automatically declassified on December 31 of the year that is 25 years from the date of origin, except as provided in paragraphs (b)–(d) and (g)–(j) of this section. If the date of origin of an individual record cannot be readily determined, the date of original classification shall be used instead.

(b) An agency head may exempt from automatic declassification under paragraph (a) of this section specific information, the release of which should clearly and demonstrably be expected to:

(1) reveal the identity of a confidential human source, a human intelligence source, a relationship with an intelligence or security service of a foreign

government or international organization, or a nonhuman intelligence source; or impair the effectiveness of an intelligence method currently in use, available for use, or under development;

(2) reveal information that would assist in the development, production, or use of weapons of mass destruction;

(3) reveal information that would impair U.S. cryptologic systems or activities;

(4) reveal information that would impair the application of state-of-the-art technology within a U.S. weapon system;

(5) reveal formally named or numbered U.S. military war plans that remain in effect, or reveal operational or tactical elements of prior plans that are contained in such active plans;

(6) reveal information, including foreign government information, that would cause serious harm to relations between the United States and a foreign government, or to ongoing diplomatic activities of the United States;

(7) reveal information that would impair the current ability of United States Government officials to protect the President, Vice President, and other protectees for whom protection services, in the interest of the national security, are authorized;

(8) reveal information that would seriously impair current national security emergency preparedness plans or reveal current vulnerabilities of systems, installations, or infrastructures relating to the national security; or

(9) violate a statute, treaty, or international agreement that does not permit the automatic or unilateral declassification of information at 25 years.

(c)(1) An agency head shall notify the Panel of any specific file series of records for which a review or assessment has determined that the information within that file series almost invariably falls within one or more of the exemption categories listed in paragraph (b) of this section and that the agency proposes to exempt from automatic declassification at 25 years.

(2) The notification shall include:

(A) a description of the file series;

(B) an explanation of why the information within the file series is almost invariably exempt from automatic declassification and why the information must remain classified for a longer period of time; and

(C) except when the information within the file series almost invariably identifies a confidential human source or a human intelligence source or key design concepts of weapons of mass destruction, a specific date or event for declassification of the information, not to exceed December 31 of the year that is 50 years from the date of origin of the records.

(3) The Panel may direct the agency not to exempt a designated file series or to declassify the information within that series at an earlier date than recommended. The agency head may appeal such a decision to the President through the National Security Advisor.

(4) File series exemptions approved by the President prior to December 31, 2008, shall remain valid without any additional agency action pending Panel review by the later of December 31, 2010, or December 31 of the year that is 10 years from the date of previous approval.

(d) The following provisions shall apply to the onset of automatic declassification:

(1) Classified records within an integral file block, as defined in this order, that are otherwise subject to automatic declassification under this section shall not be automatically declassified until December 31 of the year that is 25 years from the date of the most recent record within the file block.

(2) After consultation with the Director of the National Declassification Center (the Center) established by section 3.7 of this order and before the records are subject to automatic declassification, an agency head or senior agency official may delay automatic declassification for up to five additional years for classified information contained in media that make a review for possible declassification exemptions more difficult or costly.

(3) Other than for records that are properly exempted from automatic declassification, records containing classified information that originated with other agencies or the disclosure of which would affect the interests or activities of other agencies with respect to the classified information and could reasonably be expected to fall under one or more of the exemptions in paragraph (b) of this section shall be identified prior to the onset of automatic declassification for later referral to those agencies.

(A) The information of concern shall be referred by the Center established by section 3.7 of this order, or by the centralized facilities referred to in section 3.7(e) of this order, in a prioritized and scheduled manner determined by the Center.

(B) If an agency fails to provide a final determination on a referral made by the Center within 1 year of referral, or by the centralized facilities referred to in section 3.7(e) of this order within 3 years of referral, its equities in the referred records shall be automatically declassified.

(C) If any disagreement arises between affected agencies and the Center regarding the referral review period, the Director of the Information Security Oversight Office shall determine the appropriate period of review of referred records.

(D) Referrals identified prior to the establishment of the Center by section 3.7 of this order shall be subject to automatic declassification only in accordance with subparagraphs (d)(3)(A)–(C) of this section.

(4) After consultation with the Director of the Information Security Oversight Office, an agency head may delay automatic declassification for up to 3 years from the date of discovery of classified records that were inadvertently not reviewed prior to the effective date of automatic declassification.

(e) Information exempted from automatic declassification under this section shall remain subject to the mandatory and systematic declassification review provisions of this order.

(f) The Secretary of State shall determine when the United States should commence negotiations with the appropriate officials of a foreign government or international organization of governments to modify any treaty or international agreement that requires the classification of information contained in records affected by this section for a period longer than 25 years from the date of its creation, unless the treaty or international agreement pertains to information that may otherwise remain classified beyond 25 years under this section.

(g) The Secretary of Energy shall determine when information concerning foreign nuclear programs that was removed from the Restricted Data category in order to carry out provisions of the National Security Act of 1947, as amended, may be declassified. Unless otherwise determined, such information shall be declassified when comparable information concerning the United States nuclear program is declassified.

(h) Not later than 3 years from the effective date of this order, all records exempted from automatic declassification under paragraphs (b) and (c) of this section shall be automatically declassified on December 31 of a year that is no more than 50 years from the date of origin, subject to the following:

(1) Records that contain information the release of which should clearly and demonstrably be expected to reveal the following are exempt from automatic declassification at 50 years:

(A) the identity of a confidential human source or a human intelligence source; or

(B) key design concepts of weapons of mass destruction.

(2) In extraordinary cases, agency heads may, within 5 years of the onset of automatic declassification, propose to exempt additional specific information from declassification at 50 years.

(3) Records exempted from automatic declassification under this paragraph shall be automatically declassified on December 31 of a year that is no more than 75 years from the date of origin unless an agency head, within 5 years of that date, proposes to exempt specific information from declassification at 75 years and the proposal is formally approved by the Panel.

(i) Specific records exempted from automatic declassification prior to the establishment of the Center described in section 3.7 of this order shall be subject to the provisions of paragraph (h) of this section in a scheduled and prioritized manner determined by the Center.

(j) At least 1 year before information is subject to automatic declassification under this section, an agency head or senior agency official shall notify the Director of the Information Security Oversight Office, serving as Executive Secretary of the Panel, of any specific information that the agency proposes to exempt from automatic declassification under paragraphs (b) and (h) of this section.

(1) The notification shall include:

(A) a detailed description of the information, either by reference to information in specific records or in the form of a declassification guide;

(B) an explanation of why the information should be exempt from automatic declassification and must remain classified for a longer period of time; and

(C) a specific date or a specific and independently verifiable event for automatic declassification of specific records that contain the information proposed for exemption.

(2) The Panel may direct the agency not to exempt the information or to declassify it at an earlier date than recommended. An agency head may appeal such a decision to the President through the National Security Advisor. The information will remain classified while such an appeal is pending.

(k) For information in a file series of records determined not to have permanent historical value, the duration of classification beyond 25 years shall be the same as the disposition (destruction) date of those records in each Agency Records Control Schedule or General Records Schedule, although the duration of classification shall be extended if the record has been retained for business reasons beyond the scheduled disposition date.

Sec. 3.4. *Systematic Declassification Review.*

(a) Each agency that has originated classified information under this order or its predecessors shall establish and conduct a program for systematic declassification review for records of permanent historical value exempted from automatic declassification under section 3.3 of this order. Agencies shall prioritize their review of such records in accordance with priorities established by the Center.

(b) The Archivist shall conduct a systematic declassification review program for classified records:

(1) accessioned into the National Archives; (2) transferred to the Archivist pursuant to 44 U.S.C. 2203; and (3) for which the National Archives serves as the custodian for an agency or organization that has gone out of existence.

Sec. 3.5. *Mandatory Declassification Review.*

(a) Except as provided in paragraph (b) of this section, all information classified under this order or predecessor orders shall be subject to a review for declassification by the originating agency if:

(1) the request for a review describes the document or material containing the information with sufficient specificity to enable the agency to locate it with a reasonable amount of effort;

(2) the document or material containing the information responsive to the request is not contained within an operational file exempted from search and review, publication, and disclosure under 5 U.S.C. 552 in accordance with law; and

(3) the information is not the subject of pending litigation.

(b) Information originated by the incumbent President or the incumbent Vice President; the incumbent President's White House Staff or the incumbent Vice President's Staff; committees, commissions, or boards appointed by the incumbent President; or other entities within the Executive Office of the President that solely advise and assist the incumbent President is exempted from the provisions of paragraph (a) of this section. However, the Archivist shall have the authority to review, downgrade, and declassify papers or records of former Presidents and Vice Presidents under the control of the Archivist pursuant to 44 U.S.C. 2107, 2111, 2111 note, or 2203. Review procedures developed by the Archivist shall provide for consultation with agencies having primary subject matter interest and shall be consistent with the provisions of applicable laws or lawful agreements that pertain to the respective Presidential papers or records. Agencies with primary subject matter interest shall be notified promptly of the Archivist's decision. Any final decision by the Archivist may be appealed by the requester or an agency to the Panel. The information shall remain classified pending a prompt decision on the appeal.

(c) Agencies conducting a mandatory review for declassification shall declassify information that no longer meets the standards for classification under this order. They shall release this information unless withholding is otherwise authorized and warranted under applicable law.

(d) If an agency has reviewed the requested information for declassification within the past 2 years, the agency need not conduct another review and may instead inform the requester of this fact and the prior review decision and advise the requester of appeal rights provided under subsection (e) of this section.

(e) In accordance with directives issued pursuant to this order, agency heads shall develop procedures to process requests for the mandatory review of classified information. These procedures shall apply to information classified under this or predecessor orders. They also shall provide a means for administratively appealing a denial of a mandatory review request, and for notifying the requester of the right to appeal a final agency decision to the Panel.

(f) After consultation with affected agencies, the Secretary of Defense shall develop special procedures for the review of cryptologic information; the Director of National Intelligence shall develop special procedures for the review of information pertaining to intelligence sources, methods, and activities; and the Archivist shall develop special procedures for the review of information accessioned into the National Archives.

(g) Documents required to be submitted for prepublication review or other administrative process pursuant to an approved nondisclosure agreement are not covered by this section.

(h) This section shall not apply to any request for a review made to an element of the Intelligence Community that is made by a person other than an individual as that term is defined by 5 U.S.C. 552a(a)(2), or by a foreign government entity or any representative thereof.

Sec. 3.6. *Processing Requests and Reviews.* Notwithstanding section 4.1(i) of this order, in response to a request for information under the Freedom of Information Act, the Presidential Records Act, the Privacy Act of 1974, or the mandatory review provisions of this order:

(a) An agency may refuse to confirm or deny the existence or nonexistence of requested records whenever the fact of their existence or nonexistence is itself classified under this order or its predecessors.

(b) When an agency receives any request for documents in its custody that contain classified information that originated with other agencies or the disclosure of which would affect the interests or activities of other agencies with respect to the classified information, or identifies such documents in the process of implementing sections 3.3 or 3.4 of this order, it shall refer copies of any request and the pertinent documents to the originating agency for processing and may, after consultation with the originating agency, inform any requester of the referral unless such association is itself classified under this order or its predecessors. In cases in which the originating agency determines in writing that a response under paragraph (a) of this section is required, the referring agency shall respond to the requester in accordance with that paragraph.

(c) Agencies may extend the classification of information in records determined not to have permanent historical value or nonrecord materials, including artifacts, beyond the time frames established in sections 1.5(b) and 2.2(f) of this order, provided:

(1) the specific information has been approved pursuant to section 3.3(j) of this order for exemption from automatic declassification; and

(2) the extension does not exceed the date established in section 3.3(j) of this order.

Sec. 3.7. *National Declassification Center.* (a) There is established within the National Archives a National Declassification Center to streamline declassification processes, facilitate quality-assurance measures, and implement standardized training regarding the declassification of records determined to have permanent historical value. There shall be a Director of the Center who shall be appointed or removed by the Archivist in consultation with the Secretaries of State, Defense, Energy, and Homeland Security, the Attorney General, and the Director of National Intelligence.

(b) Under the administration of the Director, the Center shall coordinate:

(1) timely and appropriate processing of referrals in accordance with section 3.3(d)(3) of this order for accessioned Federal records and transferred presidential records.

(2) general interagency declassification activities necessary to fulfill the requirements of sections 3.3 and 3.4 of this order;

(3) the exchange among agencies of detailed declassification guidance to enable the referral of records in accordance with section 3.3(d)(3) of this order;

(4) the development of effective, transparent, and standard declassification work processes, training, and quality assurance measures;

(5) the development of solutions to declassification challenges posed by electronic records, special media, and emerging technologies;

(6) the linkage and effective utilization of existing agency databases and the use of new technologies to document and make public declassification review decisions and support declassification activities under the purview of the Center; and

(7) storage and related services, on a reimbursable basis, for Federal records containing classified national security information.

(c) Agency heads shall fully cooperate with the Archivist in the activities of the Center and shall:

(1) provide the Director with adequate and current declassification guidance to enable the referral of records in accordance with section 3.3(d)(3) of this order; and

(2) upon request of the Archivist, assign agency personnel to the Center who shall be delegated authority by the agency head to review and exempt

or declassify information originated by their agency contained in records accessioned into the National Archives, after consultation with subject-matter experts as necessary.

(d) The Archivist, in consultation with representatives of the participants in the Center and after input from the general public, shall develop priorities for declassification activities under the purview of the Center that take into account the degree of researcher interest and the likelihood of declassification.

(e) Agency heads may establish such centralized facilities and internal operations to conduct internal declassification reviews as appropriate to achieve optimized records management and declassification business processes. Once established, all referral processing of accessioned records shall take place at the Center, and such agency facilities and operations shall be coordinated with the Center to ensure the maximum degree of consistency in policies and procedures that relate to records determined to have permanent historical value.

(f) Agency heads may exempt from automatic declassification or continue the classification of their own originally classified information under section 3.3(a) of this order except that in the case of the Director of National Intelligence, the Director shall also retain such authority with respect to the Intelligence Community.

(g) The Archivist shall, in consultation with the Secretaries of State, Defense, Energy, and Homeland Security, the Attorney General, the Director of National Intelligence, the Director of the Central Intelligence Agency, and the Director of the Information Security Oversight Office, provide the National Security Advisor with a detailed concept of operations for the Center and a proposed implementing directive under section 5.1 of this order that reflects the coordinated views of the aforementioned agencies.

PART 4—SAFEGUARDING

Sec. 4.1. *General Restrictions on Access.*

(a) A person may have access to classified information provided that:

(1) a favorable determination of eligibility for access has been made by an agency head or the agency head's designee;

(2) the person has signed an approved nondisclosure agreement; and

(3) the person has a need-to-know the information.

(b) Every person who has met the standards for access to classified information in paragraph (a) of this section shall receive contemporaneous training on the proper safeguarding of classified information and on the criminal, civil, and administrative sanctions that may be imposed on an individual who fails to protect classified information from unauthorized disclosure.

(c) An official or employee leaving agency service may not remove classified information from the agency's control or direct that information be declassified in order to remove it from agency control.

(d) Classified information may not be removed from official premises without proper authorization.

(e) Persons authorized to disseminate classified information outside the executive branch shall ensure the protection of the information in a manner equivalent to that provided within the executive branch.

(f) Consistent with law, executive orders, directives, and regulations, an agency head or senior agency official or, with respect to the Intelligence Community, the Director of National Intelligence, shall establish uniform procedures to ensure that automated information systems, including networks and telecommunications systems, that collect, create, communicate, compute, disseminate, process, or store classified information:

(1) prevent access by unauthorized persons;

(2) ensure the integrity of the information; and

(3) to the maximum extent practicable, use:

(A) common information technology standards, protocols, and interfaces that maximize the availability of, and access to, the information in a form and manner that facilitates its authorized use; and

(B) standardized electronic formats to maximize the accessibility of information to persons who meet the criteria set forth in section 4.1(a) of this order.

(g) Consistent with law, executive orders, directives, and regulations, each agency head or senior agency official, or with respect to the Intelligence Community, the Director of National Intelligence, shall establish controls to ensure that classified information is used, processed, stored, reproduced, transmitted, and destroyed under conditions that provide adequate protection and prevent access by unauthorized persons.

(h) Consistent with directives issued pursuant to this order, an agency shall safeguard foreign government information under standards that provide a degree of protection at least equivalent to that required by the government or international organization of governments that furnished the information. When adequate to achieve equivalency, these standards may be less restrictive than the safeguarding standards that ordinarily apply to U.S. "Confidential" information, including modified handling and transmission and allowing access to individuals with a need-to-know who have not otherwise been cleared for access to classified information or executed an approved non-disclosure agreement.

(i)(1) Classified information originating in one agency may be disseminated to another agency or U.S. entity by any agency to which it has been made available without the consent of the originating agency, as long as the criteria for access under section 4.1(a) of this order are met, unless the originating agency has determined that prior authorization is required for such dissemination and has marked or indicated such requirement on the medium containing the classified information in accordance with implementing directives issued pursuant to this order.

(2) Classified information originating in one agency may be disseminated by any other agency to which it has been made available to a foreign government in accordance with statute, this order, directives implementing this order, direction of the President, or with the consent of the originating agency. For the purposes of this section, "foreign government" includes any element of a foreign government, or an international organization of governments, or any element thereof.

(3) Documents created prior to the effective date of this order shall not be disseminated outside any other agency to which they have been made available without the consent of the originating agency. An agency head or senior agency official may waive this requirement for specific information that originated within that agency.

(4) For purposes of this section, the Department of Defense shall be considered one agency, except that any dissemination of information regarding intelligence sources, methods, or activities shall be consistent with directives issued pursuant to section 6.2(b) of this order.

(5) Prior consent of the originating agency is not required when referring records for declassification review that contain information originating in more than one agency.

Sec. 4.2 *Distribution Controls.*

(a) The head of each agency shall establish procedures in accordance with applicable law and consistent with directives issued pursuant to this order to ensure that classified information is accessible to the maximum extent possible by individuals who meet the criteria set forth in section 4.1(a) of this order.

(b) In an emergency, when necessary to respond to an imminent threat to life or in defense of the homeland, the agency head or any designee may authorize the disclosure of classified information (including information marked pursuant to section 4.1(i)(1) of this order) to an individual or individuals who are otherwise not eligible for access. Such actions shall be taken only in accordance with directives implementing this order and any procedure issued by agencies governing the classified information, which shall be designed to minimize the classified information that is disclosed under these circumstances and the number of individuals who receive it. Information disclosed under this provision or implementing directives and procedures shall not be deemed declassified as a result of such disclosure or subsequent use by a recipient. Such disclosures shall be reported promptly to the originator of the classified information. For purposes of this section, the Director of National Intelligence may issue an implementing directive governing the emergency disclosure of classified intelligence information.

(c) Each agency shall update, at least annually, the automatic, routine, or recurring distribution mechanism for classified information that it distributes. Recipients shall cooperate fully with distributors who are updating distribution lists and shall notify distributors whenever a relevant change in status occurs.

Sec. 4.3. *Special Access Programs.* (a) Establishment of special access programs. Unless otherwise authorized by the President, only the Secretaries of State, Defense, Energy, and Homeland Security, the Attorney General, and the Director of National Intelligence, or the principal deputy of each, may create a special access program. For special access programs pertaining to intelligence sources, methods, and activities (but not including military operational, strategic, and tactical programs), this function shall be exercised by the Director of National Intelligence. These officials shall keep the number of these programs at an absolute minimum, and shall establish them only when the program is required by statute or upon a specific finding that:

(1) the vulnerability of, or threat to, specific information is exceptional; and

(2) the normal criteria for determining eligibility for access applicable to information classified at the same level are not deemed sufficient to protect the information from unauthorized disclosure.

(b) Requirements and limitations.

(1) Special access programs shall be limited to programs in which the number of persons who ordinarily will have access will be reasonably small and commensurate with the objective of providing enhanced protection for the information involved.

(2) Each agency head shall establish and maintain a system of accounting for special access programs consistent with directives issued pursuant to this order.

(3) Special access programs shall be subject to the oversight program established under section 5.4(d) of this order. In addition, the Director of the Information Security Oversight Office shall be afforded access to these programs, in accordance with the security requirements of each program, in order to perform the functions assigned to the Information Security Oversight Office under this order. An agency head may limit access to a special access program to the Director of the Information Security Oversight Office and no more than one other employee of the Information Security Oversight Office or, for special access programs that are extraordinarily sensitive and vulnerable, to the Director only.

(4) The agency head or principal deputy shall review annually each special access program to determine whether it continues to meet the requirements of this order.

(5) Upon request, an agency head shall brief the National Security Advisor, or a designee, on any or all of the agency's special access programs.

(6) For the purposes of this section, the term "agency head" refers only to the Secretaries of State, Defense, Energy, and Homeland Security, the

Attorney General, and the Director of National Intelligence, or the principal deputy of each.

(c) Nothing in this order shall supersede any requirement made by or under 10 U.S.C. 119.

Sec. 4.4. *Access by Historical Researchers and Certain Former Government Personnel.*

(a) The requirement in section 4.1(a)(3) of this order that access to classified information may be granted only to individuals who have a need-to-know the information may be waived for persons who:

(1) are engaged in historical research projects;

(2) previously have occupied senior policy-making positions to which they were appointed or designated by the President or the Vice President; or

(3) served as President or Vice President.

(b) Waivers under this section may be granted only if the agency head or senior agency official of the originating agency:

(1) determines in writing that access is consistent with the interest of the national security;

(2) takes appropriate steps to protect classified information from unauthorized disclosure or compromise, and ensures that the information is safeguarded in a manner consistent with this order; and

(3) limits the access granted to former Presidential appointees or designees and Vice Presidential appointees or designees to items that the person originated, reviewed, signed, or received while serving as a Presidential or Vice Presidential appointee or designee.

PART 5—IMPLEMENTATION AND REVIEW

Sec. 5.1. *Program Direction.* (a) The Director of the Information Security Oversight Office, under the direction of the Archivist and in consultation with the National Security Advisor, shall issue such directives as are necessary to implement this order. These directives shall be binding on the agencies. Directives issued by the Director of the Information Security Oversight Office shall establish standards for:

(1) classification, declassification, and marking principles;

(2) safeguarding classified information, which shall pertain to the handling, storage, distribution, transmittal, and destruction of and accounting for classified information;

(3) agency security education and training programs;

(4) agency self-inspection programs; and

(5) classification and declassification guides.

(b) The Archivist shall delegate the implementation and monitoring functions of this program to the Director of the Information Security Oversight Office.

(c) The Director of National Intelligence, after consultation with the heads of affected agencies and the Director of the Information Security Oversight Office, may issue directives to implement this order with respect to the protection of intelligence sources, methods, and activities. Such directives shall be consistent with this order and directives issued under paragraph (a) of this section.

Sec. 5.2. *Information Security Oversight Office.* (a) There is established within the National Archives an Information Security Oversight Office. The Archivist shall appoint the Director of the Information Security Oversight Office, subject to the approval of the President.

(b) Under the direction of the Archivist, acting in consultation with the National Security Advisor, the Director of the Information Security Oversight Office shall:

(1) develop directives for the implementation of this order;

(2) oversee agency actions to ensure compliance with this order and its implementing directives;

(3) review and approve agency implementing regulations prior to their issuance to ensure their consistency with this order and directives issued under section 5.1(a) of this order;

(4) have the authority to conduct on-site reviews of each agency's program established under this order, and to require of each agency those reports and information and other cooperation that may be necessary to fulfill its responsibilities. If granting access to specific categories of classified information would pose an exceptional national security risk, the affected agency head or the senior agency official shall submit a written justification recommending the denial of access to the President through the National Security Advisor within 60 days of the request for access. Access shall be denied pending the response;

(5) review requests for original classification authority from agencies or officials not granted original classification authority and, if deemed appropriate, recommend Presidential approval through the National Security Advisor;

(6) consider and take action on complaints and suggestions from persons within or outside the Government with respect to the administration of the program established under this order;

(7) have the authority to prescribe, after consultation with affected agencies, standardization of forms or procedures that will promote the implementation of the program established under this order;

(8) report at least annually to the President on the implementation of this order; and

(9) convene and chair interagency meetings to discuss matters pertaining to the program established by this order.

Sec. 5.3. *Interagency Security Classification Appeals Panel.*

(a) Establishment and administration.

(1) There is established an Interagency Security Classification Appeals Panel. The Departments of State, Defense, and Justice, the National Archives, the Office of the Director of National Intelligence, and the National Security Advisor shall each be represented by a senior-level representative who is a full-time or permanent part-time Federal officer or employee designated to serve as a member of the Panel by the respective agency head. The President shall designate a Chair from among the members of the Panel.

(2) Additionally, the Director of the Central Intelligence Agency may appoint a temporary representative who meets the criteria in paragraph (a)(1) of this section to participate as a voting member in all Panel deliberations and associated support activities concerning classified information originated by the Central Intelligence Agency.

(3) A vacancy on the Panel shall be filled as quickly as possible as provided in paragraph (a)(1) of this section.

(4) The Director of the Information Security Oversight Office shall serve as the Executive Secretary of the Panel. The staff of the Information Security Oversight Office shall provide program and administrative support for the Panel.

(5) The members and staff of the Panel shall be required to meet eligibility for access standards in order to fulfill the Panel's functions.

(6) The Panel shall meet at the call of the Chair. The Chair shall schedule meetings as may be necessary for the Panel to fulfill its functions in a timely manner.

(7) The Information Security Oversight Office shall include in its reports to the President a summary of the Panel's activities.

(b) Functions The Panel shall:

(1) decide on appeals by persons who have filed classification challenges under section 1.8 of this order;

(2) approve, deny, or amend agency exemptions from automatic declassification as provided in section 3.3 of this order;

(3) decide on appeals by persons or entities who have filed requests for mandatory declassification review under section 3.5 of this order; and

(4) appropriately inform senior agency officials and the public of final Panel decisions on appeals under sections 1.8 and 3.5 of this order.

(c) Rules and procedures. The Panel shall issue bylaws, which shall be published in the *Federal Register*. The bylaws shall establish the rules and procedures that the Panel will follow in accepting, considering, and issuing decisions on appeals. The rules and procedures of the Panel shall provide that the Panel will consider appeals only on actions in which:

(1) the appellant has exhausted his or her administrative remedies within the responsible agency;

(2) there is no current action pending on the issue within the Federal courts; and

(3) the information has not been the subject of review by the Federal courts or the Panel within the past 2 years.

(d) Agency heads shall cooperate fully with the Panel so that it can fulfill its functions in a timely and fully informed manner. The Panel shall report to the President through the National Security Advisor any instance in which it believes that an agency head is not cooperating fully with the Panel.

(e) The Panel is established for the sole purpose of advising and assisting the President in the discharge of his constitutional and discretionary authority to protect the national security of the United States. Panel decisions are committed to the discretion of the Panel, unless changed by the President.

(f) An agency head may appeal a decision of the Panel to the President through the National Security Advisor. The information shall remain classified pending a decision on the appeal.

Sec. 5.4. *General Responsibilities.* Heads of agencies that originate or handle classified information shall:

(a) demonstrate personal commitment and commit senior management to the successful implementation of the program established under this order;

(b) commit necessary resources to the effective implementation of the program established under this order;

(c) ensure that agency records systems are designed and maintained to optimize the appropriate sharing and safeguarding of classified information, and to facilitate its declassification under the terms of this order when it no longer meets the standards for continued classification; and

(d) designate a senior agency official to direct and administer the program, whose responsibilities shall include:

(1) overseeing the agency's program established under this order, provided an agency head may designate a separate official to oversee special access programs authorized under this order. This official shall provide a full accounting of the agency's special access programs at least annually;

(2) promulgating implementing regulations, which shall be published in the *Federal Register* to the extent that they affect members of the public;

(3) establishing and maintaining security education and training programs;

(4) establishing and maintaining an ongoing self-inspection program, which shall include the regular reviews of representative samples of the agency's

original and derivative classification actions, and shall authorize appropriate agency officials to correct misclassification actions not covered by sections 1.7(c) and 1.7(d) of this order; and reporting annually to the Director of the Information Security Oversight Office on the agency's self-inspection program;

(5) establishing procedures consistent with directives issued pursuant to this order to prevent unnecessary access to classified information, including procedures that:

(A) require that a need for access to classified information be established before initiating administrative clearance procedures; and

(B) ensure that the number of persons granted access to classified information meets the mission needs of the agency while also satisfying operational and security requirements and needs;

(6) developing special contingency plans for the safeguarding of classified information used in or near hostile or potentially hostile areas;

(7) ensuring that the performance contract or other system used to rate civilian or military personnel performance includes the designation and management of classified information as a critical element or item to be evaluated in the rating of:

(A) original classification authorities;

(B) security managers or security specialists; and

(C) all other personnel whose duties significantly involve the creation or handling of classified information, including personnel who regularly apply derivative classification markings;

(8) accounting for the costs associated with the implementation of this order, which shall be reported to the Director of the Information Security Oversight Office for publication;

(9) assigning in a prompt manner agency personnel to respond to any request, appeal, challenge, complaint, or suggestion arising out of this order that pertains to classified information that originated in a component of the agency that no longer exists and for which there is no clear successor in function; and

(10) establishing a secure capability to receive information, allegations, or complaints regarding over-classification or incorrect classification within the agency and to provide guidance to personnel on proper classification as needed.

Sec. 5.5. *Sanctions.* (a) If the Director of the Information Security Oversight Office finds that a violation of this order or its implementing directives has occurred, the Director shall make a report to the head of the agency or to the senior agency official so that corrective steps, if appropriate, may be taken.

(b) Officers and employees of the United States Government, and its contractors, licensees, certificate holders, and grantees shall be subject to appropriate sanctions if they knowingly, willfully, or negligently:

(1) disclose to unauthorized persons information properly classified under this order or predecessor orders;

(2) classify or continue the classification of information in violation of this order or any implementing directive;

(3) create or continue a special access program contrary to the requirements of this order; or

(4) contravene any other provision of this order or its implementing directives.

(c) Sanctions may include reprimand, suspension without pay, removal, termination of classification authority, loss or denial of access to classified information, or other sanctions in accordance with applicable law and agency regulation.

(d) The agency head, senior agency official, or other supervisory official shall, at a minimum, promptly remove the classification authority of any individual who demonstrates reckless disregard or a pattern of error in applying the classification standards of this order.

(e) The agency head or senior agency official shall:

(1) take appropriate and prompt corrective action when a violation or infraction under paragraph (b) of this section occurs; and

(2) notify the Director of the Information Security Oversight Office when a violation under paragraph (b)(1), (2), or (3) of this section occurs

PART 6—GENERAL PROVISIONS

Sec. 6.1. *Definitions.* For purposes of this order:

(a) "Access" means the ability or opportunity to gain knowledge of classified information.

(b) "Agency" means any "Executive agency," as defined in 5 U.S.C. 105; any "Military department" as defined in 5 U.S.C. 102; and any other entity within the executive branch that comes into the possession of classified information.

(c) "Authorized holder" of classified information means anyone who satisfies the conditions for access stated in section 4.1(a) of this order.

(d) "Automated information system" means an assembly of computer hardware, software, or firmware configured to collect, create, communicate, compute, disseminate, process, store, or control data or information.

(e) "Automatic declassification" means the declassification of information based solely upon:

(1) the occurrence of a specific date or event as determined by the original classification authority; or

(2) the expiration of a maximum time frame for duration of classification established under this order.

(f) "Classification" means the act or process by which information is determined to be classified information.

(g) "Classification guidance" means any instruction or source that prescribes the classification of specific information.

(h) "Classification guide" means a documentary form of classification guidance issued by an original classification authority that identifies the elements of information regarding a specific subject that must be classified and establishes the level and duration of classification for each such element.

(i) "Classified national security information" or "classified information" means information that has been determined pursuant to this order or any predecessor order to require protection against unauthorized disclosure and is marked to indicate its classified status when in documentary form.

(j) "Compilation" means an aggregation of preexisting unclassified items of information.

(k) "Confidential source" means any individual or organization that has provided, or that may reasonably be expected to provide, information to the United States on matters pertaining to the national security with the expectation that the information or relationship, or both, are to be held in confidence.

(l) "Damage to the national security" means harm to the national defense or foreign relations of the United States from the unauthorized disclosure of information, taking into consideration such aspects of the information as the sensitivity, value, utility, and provenance of that information.

(m) "Declassification" means the authorized change in the status of information from classified information to unclassified information.

(n) "Declassification guide" means written instructions issued by a declassification authority that describes the elements of information regarding a specific subject that may be declassified and the elements that must remain classified.

(o) "Derivative classification" means the incorporating, paraphrasing, restating, or generating in new form information that is already classified, and marking the newly developed material consistent with the classification markings that apply to the source information. Derivative classification includes the classification of information based on classification guidance. The duplication or reproduction of existing classified information is not derivative classification.

(p) "Document" means any recorded information, regardless of the nature of the medium or the method or circumstances of recording.

(q) "Downgrading" means a determination by a declassification authority that information classified and safeguarded at a specified level shall be classified and safeguarded at a lower level.

(r) "File series" means file units or documents arranged according to a filing system or kept together because they relate to a particular subject or function, result from the same activity, document a specific kind of transaction, take a particular physical form, or have some other relationship arising out of their creation, receipt, or use, such as restrictions on access or use.

(s) "Foreign government information" means:

(1) information provided to the United States Government by a foreign government or governments, an international organization of governments, or any element thereof, with the expectation that the information, the source of the information, or both, are to be held in confidence;

(2) information produced by the United States Government pursuant to or as a result of a joint arrangement with a foreign government or governments, or an international organization of governments, or any element thereof, requiring that the information, the arrangement, or both, are to be held in confidence; or

(3) information received and treated as "foreign government information" under the terms of a predecessor order.

(t) "Information" means any knowledge that can be communicated or documentary material, regardless of its physical form or characteristics, that is owned by, is produced by or for, or is under the control of the United States Government.

(u) "Infraction" means any knowing, willful, or negligent action contrary to the requirements of this order or its implementing directives that does not constitute a "violation," as defined below.

(v) "Integral file block" means a distinct component of a file series, as defined in this section, that should be maintained as a separate unit in order to ensure the integrity of the records. An integral file block may consist of a set of records covering either a specific topic or a range of time, such as a Presidential administration or a 5-year retirement schedule within a specific file series that is retired from active use as a group. For purposes of automatic declassification, integral file blocks shall contain only records dated within 10 years of the oldest record in the file block.

(w) "Integrity" means the state that exists when information is unchanged from its source and has not been accidentally or intentionally modified, altered, or destroyed.

(x) "Intelligence" includes foreign intelligence and counterintelligence as defined by Executive Order 12333 of December 4, 1981, as amended, or by a successor order.

(y) "Intelligence activities" means all activities that elements of the Intelligence Community are authorized to conduct pursuant to law or Executive Order 12333, as amended, or a successor order.

(z) "Intelligence Community" means an element or agency of the U.S. Government identified in or designated pursuant to section 3(4) of the National Security Act of 1947, as amended, or section 3.5(h) of Executive Order 12333, as amended.

(aa) "Mandatory declassification review" means the review for declassification of classified information in response to a request for declassification that meets the requirements under section 3.5 of this order.

(bb) "Multiple sources" means two or more source documents, classification guides, or a combination of both.

(cc) "National security" means the national defense or foreign relations of the United States.

(dd) "Need-to-know" means a determination within the executive branch in accordance with directives issued pursuant to this order that a prospective recipient requires access to specific classified information in order to perform or assist in a lawful and authorized governmental function.

(ee) 'Network" means a system of two or more computers that can exchange data or information.

(ff) "Original classification" means an initial determination that information requires, in the interest of the national security, protection against unauthorized disclosure.

(gg) "Original classification authority" means an individual authorized in writing, either by the President, the Vice President, or by agency heads or other officials designated by the President, to classify information in the first instance.

(hh) "Records" means the records of an agency and Presidential papers or Presidential records, as those terms are defined in title 44, United States Code, including those created or maintained by a government contractor, licensee, certificate holder, or grantee that are subject to the sponsoring agency's control under the terms of the contract, license, certificate, or grant.

(ii) "Records having permanent historical value" means Presidential papers or Presidential records and the records of an agency that the Archivist has determined should be maintained permanently in accordance with title 44, United States Code.

(jj) "Records management" means the planning, controlling, directing, organizing, training, promoting, and other managerial activities involved with respect to records creation, records maintenance and use, and records disposition in order to achieve adequate and proper documentation of the policies and transactions of the Federal Government and effective and economical management of agency operations.

(kk) "Safeguarding" means measures and controls that are prescribed to protect classified information.

(ll) "Self-inspection" means the internal review and evaluation of individual agency activities and the agency as a whole with respect to the implementation of the program established under this order and its implementing directives.

(mm) "Senior agency official" means the official designated by the agency head under section 5.4(d) of this order to direct and administer the agency's program under which information is classified, safeguarded, and declassified.

(nn) "Source document" means an existing document that contains classified information that is incorporated, paraphrased, restated, or generated in new form into a new document.

(oo) "Special access program" means a program established for a specific class of classified information that imposes safeguarding and access requirements that exceed those normally required for information at the same classification level.

(pp) "Systematic declassification review" means the review for declassification of classified information contained in records that have been determined by the Archivist to have permanent historical value in accordance with title 44, United States Code.

(qq) "Telecommunications" means the preparation, transmission, or communication of information by electronic means.

(rr) "Unauthorized disclosure" means a communication or physical transfer of classified information to an unauthorized recipient.

(ss) "U.S. entity" includes:

(1) State, local, or tribal governments;

(2) State, local, and tribal law enforcement and firefighting entities;

(3) public health and medical entities;

(4) regional, state, local, and tribal emergency management entities, including State Adjutants General and other appropriate public safety entities; or

(5) private sector entities serving as part of the nation's Critical Infrastructure/Key Resources.

(tt) "Violation" means:

(1) any knowing, willful, or negligent action that could reasonably be expected to result in an unauthorized disclosure of classified information;

(2) any knowing, willful, or negligent action to classify or continue the classification of information contrary to the requirements of this order or its implementing directives; or

(3) any knowing, willful, or negligent action to create or continue a special access program contrary to the requirements of this order.

(uu) "Weapons of mass destruction" means any weapon of mass destruction as defined in 50 U.S.C. 1801(p).

Sec. 6.2. *General Provisions.* (a) Nothing in this order shall supersede any requirement made by or under the Atomic Energy Act of 1954, as amended, or the National Security Act of 1947, as amended. "Restricted Data" and "Formerly Restricted Data" shall be handled, protected, classified, downgraded, and declassified in conformity with the provisions of the Atomic Energy Act of 1954, as amended, and regulations issued under that Act.

(b) The Director of National Intelligence may, with respect to the Intelligence Community and after consultation with the heads of affected departments and agencies, issue such policy directives and guidelines as the Director of National Intelligence deems necessary to implement this order with respect to the classification and declassification of all intelligence and intelligence-related information, and for access to and dissemination of all intelligence and intelligence-related information, both in its final form and in the form when initially gathered. Procedures or other guidance issued by Intelligence Community element heads shall be in accordance with such policy directives or guidelines issued by the Director of National Intelligence. Any such policy directives or guidelines issued by the Director of National Intelligence shall be in accordance with directives issued by the Director of the Information Security Oversight Office under section 5.1(a) of this order.

(c) The Attorney General, upon request by the head of an agency or the Director of the Information Security Oversight Office, shall render an interpretation of this order with respect to any question arising in the course of its administration.

(d) Nothing in this order limits the protection afforded any information by other provisions of law, including the Constitution, Freedom of Information Act exemptions, the Privacy Act of 1974, and the National Security Act of 1947, as amended. This order is not intended to and does not create any right or benefit, substantive or procedural, enforceable at law by a party against the United States, its departments, agencies, or entities, its officers, employees, or agents, or any other person. The foregoing is in addition to the specific provisos set forth in sections 1.1(b), 3.1(c) and 5.3(e) of this order.

(e) Nothing in this order shall be construed to obligate action or otherwise affect functions by the Director of the Office of Management and Budget relating to budgetary, administrative, or legislative proposals.

(f) This order shall be implemented subject to the availability of appropriations.

(g) Executive Order 12958 of April 17, 1995, and amendments thereto, including Executive Order 13292 of March 25, 2003, are hereby revoked as of the effective date of this order.

Sec. 6.3. *Effective Date.* This order is effective 180 days from the date of this order, except for sections 1.7, 3.3, and 3.7, which are effective immediately.

Sec. 6.4. *Publication.* The Archivist of the United States shall publish this Executive Order in the *Federal Register*.

THE WHITE HOUSE,
December 29, 2010.